Designing
Surveys
That
Work!

Designing
Surveys
That
Work!

A Step-by-Step Guide

Susan J. Thomas

CORWIN PRESS, INC.
A Sage Publications Company
Thousand Oaks, California

For information address:

Corwin Press, Inc.
A Sage Publications Company
2455 Teller Road
Thousand Oaks, California 91320
E-mail: order@corwinpress.com

SAGE Publications Ltd.
6 Bonhill Street
London EC2A 4PU
United Kingdom

SAGE Publications India Pvt. Ltd.
M-32 Market
Greater Kailash I
New Delhi 110 048 India

Printed in the United States of America

Library of Congress Cataloging-in-Publication Data

Thomas, Susan J.
    Designing surveys that work! A step-by-step guide / by Susan
J. Thomas
      p. cm.
    ISBN 0-8039-6851-5 (cloth: acid-free paper)
    ISBN 0-8039-6852-3 (pbk.: acid-free paper)
    1. Social sciences—Research. 2. Social surveys. I. Title.
H62 .T447 1999
001.4'33—dc21   98-51239

99 00 01 02 03 04 05 7 6 5 4 3 2 1

Corwin Editorial Assistant:	Julia Parnell
Production Editor:	Denise Santoyo
Editorial Assistant:	Patricia Zeman
Typesetter/Designer:	Lynn Miyata
Cover Designer:	Tracy E. Miller

Contents

Preface

Increasingly often, educators are being asked to provide information on which to base decisions. Surveys can be an effective means to gather such information. Creating a survey that asks the right questions at the appropriate level for the intended audience is a difficult and challenging task. *Designing Surveys That Work! A Step-by-Step Guide* was created to support those educators who want to create high-quality surveys and be confident that the data they gather will be useful.

Why Was This Guide Developed?

This Guide was developed over a 10-year period with input from hundreds of graduate students taking classes in research. The majority of the students in these classes were practicing teachers and school administrators. One of the course requirements was the creation and administration of a survey. Textbooks describing survey research focused on the research portion rather than the survey creation process. The Guide began as a series of class handouts with suggestions and guidelines for creating a survey and evolved to include examples of both surveys and cover letters. The first version of the Guide was created 3 years ago and provided to students who deemed it critical to the success of their survey projects. Since then, it has been revised to incorporate suggestions from the teachers and school administrators taking these graduate classes.

What Are the Unique Features of the Guide?

The suggestions and input from the teachers, school administrators, and other practicing professionals who took the research classes led to the inclusion of several unique features of the Guide:

- Step-by-step guidance for educators who are creating surveys

- Survey development process divided into phases, with details and examples of how to complete each phase

- Worksheets included with many of the phases

- Each phase concluding with a checklist

- Each phase containing numerous examples, beginning with examples of research questions and objectives that will guide the development of the survey, to many examples of survey items and cover letters, gatekeeper letters, and ways to present the results of the survey data

- Extensive review checklists to help ensure that you've got a high-quality survey

- Suggestions for a variety of ways to gather survey data, including mailed surveys, face-to-face data collection, E-mail distribution, and Web-based survey distribution

Who Should Read the Guide?

Teachers, school administrators, school board members, and community members involved in school activities all have information needs. In many cases, the data required for decision making can be gathered with custom-designed surveys. Most educators do not have the time to take a class to learn how to create a survey or the resources available to hire a consultant to create a survey for them. The Guide is designed to help these educators create high-quality surveys to meet their needs for information.

The Guide will also be useful to graduate students designing surveys as part of their thesis work. Professors of educational research will find the Guide a useful adjunct to research textbooks. Students will be able to create surveys for their class projects with a minimum amount of support and mentoring from their professors.

Overview of Scope and Organization of the Guide

Phase 1: Planning

Successful projects are those that have planning elements included as a central part of the project. Planning is critical to the success of a survey project. Planning includes identifying and narrowing the topic of the survey project, creating specific objectives that will guide the development of the survey tool, identifying the target audience (persons who will respond to the survey), identifying colleagues who will work with you on the survey project, and creating a time line for the project.

Phase 2: Developing the Survey

During this phase of the project, the survey tool is created. There are many decisions to be made in this phase, including the type of items, the length of the survey, the kinds of responses the participants will provide and how these responses will be scored, and the overall look and feel of the survey (formatting issues). At the end of this phase, you will have a draft survey tool.

Phase 3: Obtaining the Respondents

After you've developed your survey tool, you'll need respondents. Phase 3 guides you through the steps of contacting the appropriate gatekeepers to obtain permission to use your survey to gather the information you need. There are many sample letters included to help you create cover letters that will get results. Phase 3 also includes a discussion of informed consent and ethical issues that may arise when surveys are used.

Phase 4: Preparing for Data Collection

Before sending (or distributing) the survey to many potential respondents, you should pilot test the survey tool. This important step helps ensure that the directions and all items are clear and understandable to the target audience. You may need to make some minor revisions after the pilot testing, and then you're ready to duplicate the survey (or prepare the survey for electronic distribution). Another step in this phase is creating a list of all persons who will receive the survey. (In Phase 3, you obtained access to the respondents; here, you will create a master list of all persons who will receive the survey.)

Phase 5: Collecting the Survey Data

Attention to detail is critical in this phase, as all of the pieces of the survey project must come together. The cover letter, any incentives, and a copy of the survey must be provided to each potential respondent. Suggestions are provided for increasing the response rate, as well as for protecting the confidentiality of the data.

Phase 6: Summarizing the Survey Data

How can the information gathered from the surveys be put into a format that is usable and friendly? What are the critical questions that must be answered (i.e., why did you collect survey data)? Unless you are preparing a formal research report, it's likely that results can best be summarized with charts and graphs. An example of a short survey, its results, and a suggested way of presenting the results are included in this phase. Although analyses of survey data may use complex statistical techniques, those techniques are beyond the scope of this Guide.

Acknowledgments

Mildred Murray Ward, EdD, and Dr. Paul Burden provided insightful suggestions for making this book even more user-friendly. Their thoughtful suggestions are gratefully acknowledged.

Special thanks to Dr. Sandra Stein, Professor of Education at Rider University, a colleague and friend who encouraged me to put this Guide into a format available to educators and other professionals. She also provided the questions that form the basis of the review process included in Phases 2 and 3. Currently, her classes in research methods are using a version of the Guide, and her students continue to give her accolades for making it available to them. Many of the examples in the Guide are based on suggestions and requests over the past 10 years from students in her classes as well as my own.

About the Author

Susan J. Thomas is Senior Performance Consultant with IBM Learning Services, the Performance and Competency Management Consulting Group. She works with the Performance Measurement Service Line, which provides consulting services to companies in the areas of skills competency analysis, certification test development and skills assessment, survey development, and training evaluation.

Prior to joining the IBM Corporation, she was a measurement statistician and test development specialist with the Educational Testing Service. She also was an adjunct professor at Rider University where she taught graduate courses in research methods, testing and measurement for teachers, basic statistics, and authentic assessment.

Previously, she was a faculty member at the University of Illinois, Urbana-Champaign, and the Florida State University, where she taught courses in measurement, in research design, and in various areas of educational and developmental psychology. She has directed numerous funded research projects, has presented extensively at the annual meetings of the American Educational Research Association and the National Council for Measurement in Education, and has served as a Divisional Vice President of the American Educational Research Association.

She has published several journal articles, as well as a book titled *Evaluation Without Fear* with coauthor Roger Kaufman. She conducts workshops for teachers on topics related to assessment and has developed many training guides for these workshops. She did her undergraduate work at the University of Wisconsin-Eau Claire and received her PhD from Purdue University.

Phase I

Planning the Survey Project

———— •◆• ————

A small group of teachers requests computer software for their classes. How many other teachers in the district could also use the software? What training will teachers need to use the software?

A librarian indicates that additional Internet access is needed. How many students are currently using the Internet at the library? What implications might this have for extended library hours? Can community members also use this service?

The PTA (Parent-Teachers Association) wants to hold a fundraising event. What type of event will provide the greatest benefit? Which members will be willing to work at the event? How much planning time will be needed? What is the expected revenue?

———— •◆• ————

As you can see from these examples, educators can use surveys to gather information about many different topics and for many different reasons. A theme underlying these examples is the need for information to make a decision.

A carefully constructed survey can provide information for many types of projects, such as the following:

- Identifying needs (needs assessment)

  What kinds of inservice workshops and seminars should be offered next year?

  What advanced courses should be offered to seniors next year?

- Determining opinions, attitudes, and beliefs

  What are parents' attitudes about year-round schools?

  Do teachers believe their instructional skills are effective?

- Identifying interests

  Which class activities should be kept and which should be changed?

  What musical interests do students have?

- Identifying feelings, perceptions

  How do students feel about homework assignments that require Internet-based research?

  How do parents perceive the value of magnet schools?

- Describing behaviors

  How often do students use various school facilities, such as the library, resource center, computer lab, sports equipment, and pool?

  What kinds of reading-related activities do parents of early elementary students use with their children?

The key to creating a useful survey is to know what kind of information you need—and then to take the time necessary to do the planning and groundwork that are essential to the success of any survey project.

Planning: An Essential Ingredient

Remember the last time you went on vacation? And the planning you did before you left? What would have happened if you had done *no* planning before you left . . . just got in your car and headed down the highway? Or boarded any plane at the airport?

Just as planning your vacation helps ensure a good time, selecting the destination, making hotel reservations, checking out activities to do while you're there . . . planning your survey project helps ensure its success.

Figure 1.1. Good planning helps ensure success!

Successful people spend quality time planning—often, more time in careful and thoughtful planning than in executing the project. Did you spend more time planning your vacation than you did traveling? I know I often do . . . and I have a great time on vacation because of the planning. The more thorough your work now, the more efficient and effective will be your efforts for the rest of the project. And yes, you are more likely to do things right the first time and to get the kind of data that will be useful to you!

The planning phase consists of four activities:

- Identifying a topic

- Writing a research question and objectives

- Selecting the appropriate target group

- Developing a time line for the project

Identifying a Topic

Identify a general topic area about which you need to gather data to make a decision or about which you want more information, perhaps for planning purposes.

Read some research articles on your topic, focusing on research studies that use surveys or interviews. What kinds of questions did the researchers pose?

BOX 1.1

Hint: You might want to make copies of one or two articles and refer to them as you work on your survey project.

Brainstorm the kinds of information you'd like to know about the topic, working with colleagues.

Focus on two or three related, narrow topics from the research or your experience (or both) in the topic area. (Too many topics will make the survey too long, and folks are less likely to take the time to respond!)

You're ready for the next step, creating the research question and the objectives that will guide the development of the rest of your survey project.

Writing the Research Question and Objectives

The *research question* is a general statement of the overall focus of the survey project. Here is a sample:

What are some of the perceptions of minority group social relationships in middle school students?

Objectives flow from the research question. They are more specific and focused and provide specific guidance to you as you write items for your survey. Figure 1.2 depicts the relationship of the research question and objectives.

Here follow some sample objectives and survey items.

- To describe how minority adolescents perceive themselves:
    1. I am usually well organized.
    2. I have a good sense of humor.

- To describe how minority adolescents perceive their nonminority peers:

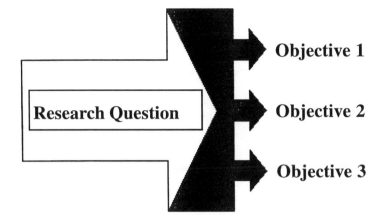

Figure 1.2. The relationship of the research question and objectives.

1. Most white kids are treated better at school than I am.

2. I think most white kids are prejudiced.

■ To describe minority adolescents' relationships with their non-minority peers:

1. White kids at my school include me in their social plans.

2. I try to avoid talking with white kids at my school.

BOX 1.2

Guidelines for Writing Clear Objectives

1. Focus each objective on one concept or idea.
2. Do not use the word *and*. (Be careful—if one of your objectives uses *and*, it probably is really two objectives.)
3. Tie each objective to the research question.
4. Demographic information is *not* one of your objectives.

Use the following worksheet (Form 1.1) to practice connecting your research question with your objectives.

FORM 1.1

Worksheet for Research Question and Objectives

State your research question here:

_____

_____

_____

_____

_____

Objective 1:

_____

_____

_____

_____

Objective 2:

_____

_____

_____

_____

Objective 3:

_____

_____

_____

_____

Figure 1.3. Target the right group of respondents!

Selecting the Appropriate Target Group

The persons from whom you will gather information for your survey project are called the *target group*. When you wrote your research question, you probably envisioned a particular group of people who might participate in your study. Were these middle school students? Participants in counseling sessions? Parents with children ready to enter school? Persons with particular kinds of experiences, such as being a parent or a grandparent? Or teachers who have taken a particular seminar or workshop?

Usually, there will be a limited number of people who can provide the information you require. To gather information to answer the sample research question given at the beginning of the chapter, we'd need to work with minority middle school students who attend an integrated school. No other group would have the necessary experiences to provide the answers to our survey items.

If you are asking about opinions or attitudes, be sure the respondents have had the appropriate experience or knowledge (or both) to form an opinion or attitude about a topic. Use Form 1.2, which follows, to practice selecting your target group.

BOX 1.3

Note: All persons who participate in your study must provide informed consent in addition to the various permissions already mentioned. See Chapter 3 for details.

FORM 1.2

Worksheet for Selecting Your Target Group

Describe the people from whom you will gather your data. Be specific . . . ages, demographic characteristics, experiences.

_____

_____

_____

_____

Why do you believe this particular group of people will be able to provide you with the appropriate information?

_____

_____

_____

_____

Where will you find these people?

_____

_____

_____

_____

How will you gain access to these people? Be specific—from whom will you need permission? How will you obtain this permission?

_____

_____

_____

_____

_____

Do these people have some characteristic that will require special efforts to include them in the study? For example, school-age children will require permission from their parents or guardians, as well as school personnel. Persons in special settings (counseling centers, nursing homes, fraternities and sororities) will require permission from the cognizant administrator.

_____

_____

_____

_____

_____

TABLE 1.1 Sample Time Line

The date the information from the survey will be needed: March 31

Estimated time to accomplish tasks: 13 weeks
  (based on the time line that follows)

Project Start Date: January 1

Tasks and Time Estimates

■ Conducting the planning phase (2 weeks)

■ Obtaining permission to conduct the study, if necessary
  (1-2 weeks)

■ Creating and pilot testing the survey (4 weeks)

■ Obtaining permission for access to participants, if necessary
  (1-2 weeks)

■ Creating plans for data collection (1 week)

■ Producing and distributing the surveys (1 week)

■ Receiving the completed surveys, doing follow-up as necessary
  (4 weeks)

■ Summarizing the data (2 weeks)

■ Preparing the findings of the survey project (1 week)

Developing a Time Line for the Project

Every survey is created to gather information for a specific purpose. That purpose is most likely time sensitive—there is an implied (or real!) deadline when the information must be available.

An important part of the planning phase is identifying the important project milestones to help ensure that you will have the information from the survey when you need it. The sample time line (Table 1.1) is based on the assumption that educators creating surveys will be working on the project during the school year and cannot devote full time to the project.

TABLE 1.2 Project Plan for a Survey Project

	Weeks												
0	1	2	3	4	5	6	7	8	9	10	11	12	13

A. Initiate project
B. Planning
C. Obtain permission
D. Create survey
E. Create data collection plan
F. Produce survey
G. Distribute survey
Summarize data H.
Prepare final report I.

KEY

A. Initiate project.
B. Conduct planning phase.
C. Obtain appropriate permissions—for conducting the study and for contacting the participants.
D. Create and pilot test the survey.
E. Create plan for data collection.
F. Produce the survey.
G. Distribute the survey, follow-up as necessary, and receive the responses.
H. Summarize the survey results.
I. Prepare the final report.

Some tasks may be conducted concurrently, and for others, completion of the prior task is required. For example, if permission to conduct the study is necessary, this important task should be completed before you put too much effort into creating the survey. The following sample project plan corresponding to the estimated time line demonstrates how this can work. The last page of this chapter is a checklist for Phase 1 (Form 1.3) that you can use to make sure you've covered all the bases.

FORM 1.3

Phase 1 Checklist

____ Will the topic you identified provide the basis for developing a survey to gather the information you need?

____ Does the research question capture the essence of your concern/interest/need for information?

____ Do the objectives clearly link to (and flow from) the research question?

____ Does the target group you've identified have the information required to provide valid information?

____ Have you identified interested colleagues to collaborate with you on the project?

____ Have you developed a time line for the project?

Phase 2

Developing the Survey

In this phase of the project, you'll create five more pieces of your survey project:

- Items for each of the objectives
- Response options
- Scoring plans
- Demographic items
- Survey format

All of these pieces are interrelated.

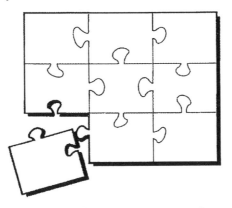

Figure 2.1. All the pieces of the Survey Project fit together!

Types of Items

BOX 2.1

An *item* is an element of a survey designed to elicit a response.

Responses to survey items can be a series of choices (*fixed response*) or the opportunity to create a response (*open response*). Both types of items and response modes can be used in a survey project, depending on the information required.

- Open-response and fixed-response items provide somewhat different types of information.

- Open-response items ask the respondent to *create* an answer. Toward the end of the chapter is a description of the process of creating high-quality open-response items.

- Fixed-response items provide choices to respondents who must *select* one of the choices you provide. Several fixed-response formats are described in the following discussion.

Fixed-Response Formats for Survey Items

Fixed-response items can be checklists, rating scales, semantic differential scales, or ranking formats. The type of items you include in your survey (and the type of responses that go with these items) will depend on your research question: What do you want to know? If your survey project will be relatively short, we recommend that you use only one type of fixed-response question. Longer surveys can use a variety of formats, matching the format to the purpose of the item.

Adjective Checklists

Adjective checklists are used to gather information about feelings. Respondents indicate their feelings about a topic, experience, or concept by circling or underlining the appropriate adjectives, as demonstrated in the following example.

Circle each word that describes how you feel about attending information sessions about how to use the library.

Unnecessary	Upsetting	Needed	Informative
Inconvenient	Important	Frustrating	Unpleasant
Practical	Useful	Worthless	Interesting

Adjective checklists are relatively simple to construct and consist of directions and a list of 12 to 16 adjectives. There should be an equal number of negative and positive adjectives, and the adjectives should be randomly ordered.

Use of Adjective Checklists

Adjective checklists can be used as a research tool before and after an intervention. For example, the adjective checklist just given can be used before the library orientation, to gauge feelings about attending such an activity, and after, to determine whether feelings changed as a result of learning the new information. Or, if you are conducting a series of group counseling sessions or introducing a new activity in your classroom, you might want to use an adjective checklist before and after to see if there were changes.

Scoring Adjective Checklists

Scoring is done by counting the number of times each adjective is chosen. When you use the survey before and after an event as has been described, count the total number of positive adjectives before and after the event, and compare the two.

As an alternative, if you would like more detail, you can count the number of times *each* adjective was chosen before and then count the times each adjective was chosen after, and compare the two.

Adjective Checklists can also be used to describe feelings at a particular point in time by administering the checklist only once.

Advantages of the Adjective Checklist:

■ Easy to create

■ Can be used in a variety of settings and for many different topics

■ Can be used with many different participant groups: Carefully constructed adjective checklists can be used with young children as well as older students and adults

Limitation:

■ Respondents cannot express *degrees* of feeling about a topic.

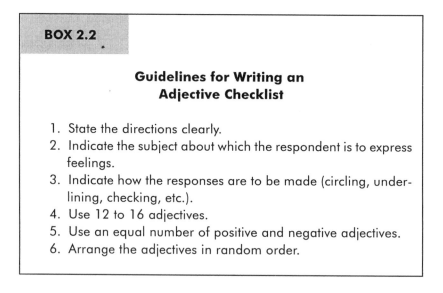

BOX 2.2

Guidelines for Writing an
Adjective Checklist

1. State the directions clearly.
2. Indicate the subject about which the respondent is to express feelings.
3. Indicate how the responses are to be made (circling, underlining, checking, etc.).
4. Use 12 to 16 adjectives.
5. Use an equal number of positive and negative adjectives.
6. Arrange the adjectives in random order.

Behavior Checklists

Behavior checklists are used to determine what experiences respondents have had, what activities they've participated in, or what activities they are interested in trying. Here's an example:

When you did the Planning Phase for your survey project, which of the following activities, if any, did you do? Please check all that apply.

_____ Obtained permission to conduct the survey from my school district.

_____ Formed a task force to work on the survey project.

_____ Read one or more journal articles about my topic.

_____ Obtained sample surveys from colleagues in other school districts.

_____ Asked a colleague for help locating resources for my survey project.

An important difference between adjective checklists and behavior checklists is that in the behavior checklist, respondents indicate what they have done, rather than what their feelings are about something. Knowing whether a person has done certain activities is often important, but we know only *whether* they've participated in the activity . . . not how often, how much they enjoyed the activity, or whether participating in the activity helped them accomplish some goal.

Scoring Behavior Checklists

Behavior checklists are scored similarly to adjective checklists: Count the number of times each response was chosen. Like the adjective checklists, behavior checklists can be used to describe responses at a particular point in time, or by administering the checklist at different times, it can indicate changes in behavior over time. Results are often reported as percentages or as tables or graphs.

Advantage of the Behavior Checklist:

■ Provides information about the respondent's experiences

Limitation:

■ No information is provided about frequency of the behavior, whether the respondent enjoyed the activity, and so forth.

BOX 2.3

Guidelines for Writing a Behavior Checklist

1. State the directions clearly.
2. Indicate the general behavior or activity being studied.
3. Specify the time period for the behavior in the directions.
4. Describe each behavior or activity in concrete, specific terms.

Practice Activity 1:

Here are two different ways to phrase the directions for a behavior checklist. Which one follows the guidelines?

Which resources have you recently used in your research?

Indicate whether you used each of the following resources in your research during the current semester.

The second set of directions is better because it clearly specifies the time period in which the behavior might have occurred. The word *recently* in the first set of instructions is open to the interpretation of the respondent and may cover this semester or any time during the person's career.

Practice Activity 2:

Which of the following two responses will provide more useful information?

Response 1: During the past month, in which of the following leisure activities did you participate?

_____ Go to a movie

_____ Have dinner with friends

_____ Watch TV

_____ Go for a walk

_____ Go shopping

Response 2: Did you participate in any leisure activities in the past month?

Response 1 provides more useful information because you will know the kinds of activities the person chose to do in his or her leisure time. Although Response 2 does specify a time period, "any leisure activities" is very broad and may be defined differently by each respondent. One person may consider shopping a leisure-time activity, whereas another thinks it's a lot of work.

Ranking Format

Asking respondents to rank items based on a common feature allows educators to learn about preferences, interests, opinions, usefulness (of something), importance, and so forth. The following example demonstrates.

Please rank the following PTA fundraising activities in terms of their potential for success in our community. Assign "1" to the activity you believe will be the most successful, "2" to the activity you believe will be second most successful, and so on.

Activity	Ranking
Car wash	_____
Bake sale	_____
Silent auction	_____
Concert	_____
Dinner dance	_____

Asking respondents to rank items forces them to indicate priority. In the example given, respondents rank the potential for success by indicating which activity they believe will be most successful, next most successful, and so on, until all items are ranked.

A ranking format can be used whenever you want information about the respondent's perception of the relative standing of a set of items, activities, interests, and so forth.

Scoring

Items with a ranking format can be scored by averaging the ranks for each item. In the example given, each of the five activities will have an average ranking, and based on this information, the activity ranked as having the greatest probability of success can be identified.

Advantages of the Ranking Format:

- It can determine the relative position or ranking of something
- Lists of things to rank are relatively easy to create

Limitation:

- It does not permit the determination of intensity of feelings or beliefs. For example, among the fundraising activities we listed, the respondent may not believe that any will be particularly successful so ranked as the first choice the one he or she thought least likely to fail.

BOX 2.4

Guidelines for Creating Ranking-Format Items

1. State the directions clearly.
2. Indicate the scale to be used to the ranking—importance, likelihood of success, degree of interest, and so on.
3. Indicate whether the highest (e.g., most successful) is ranked 1 or 5 (in our example with 5 items to rank).
4. Use only one scale with each set of ranking-format items.
5. Describe each activity or entity to be ranked clearly and concisely.

Rating Scales

Rating scales are useful for:

■ Gathering information about the *degree* to which a person finds something interesting, satisfying, helpful (or some other adjective)

■ Measuring attitudes, opinions, perceptions, and beliefs

■ Determining how frequently a person participates in certain activities

An important advantage of a rating scale is that it permits a person to respond on a continuum rather than completely endorsing (or not endorsing) something.

Ranking or Rating?

An important difference between ranking-format items and rating scales is that ranking provides information about relative standing, whereas rating scales provide information about intensity, frequency, degree of interest, degree of agreement, and so on. If the information about the potential for success of various fundraising activities were gathered using a rating scale, we might learn that respondents did not think that any of the activities listed would be successful in their community.

A sample rating scale for activities follows:

Sample Rating Scale for Activities

Please indicate how useful you found each of the following learning activities in preparing your survey project by circling the letter corresponding to your choice.

A = Not at all useful
B = A little useful
C = Somewhat useful
D = Quite useful
E = Very useful

Reading articles reporting survey research	A	B	C	D	E
Working with colleagues	A	B	C	D	E
Using this instructional manual	A	B	C	D	E
Using other surveys as models	A	B	C	D	E
Obtaining information from the Internet	A	B	C	D	E

Rating Scales for Young Children

Rating scales can be used with children in the early elementary grades if the items are carefully constructed and not overly complicated. In most cases, the items must be read to the children. Responses may be faces, such as those shown, to indicate feelings or agreement.

How do you feel when you are asked to help a classmate?   ☺   😐   ☹
                                                              Happy   OK   Sad

Responses can also be boxes or circles to indicate how much respondents like something or are interested in something.

How much do you enjoy reading time in the library?   ☐   ☐   ☐
                                                      Like it   Like it   Like it
                                                      a little   somewhat   a lot

Likert-Type Rating Scales

Many years ago, a psychologist named Rensis Likert developed a rating scale for use in measuring attitudes. His scale had five points, ranging from *strongly agree* to *strongly disagree*. Other researchers have built on his work, using more (or fewer) than five rating points and other rating anchors, such as *satisfaction, frequency, similarity to self,* and so on.

BOX 2.5

A *rating anchor* provides definitions of each of the scale points. In this example, the words following each of the letters are the anchors for the scale. You may use different anchors if you wish.

A = Strongly agree
B = Agree
C = Neither agree nor disagree
D = Disagree
E = Strongly disagree

Because most people use Likert-type rating scales for their survey projects, I will provide more detail about the construction of these scales. In the guidelines that follow, each point is demonstrated with comparative examples.

BOX 2.6

Items for rating scales contain two parts: the *stem*—the part of the item that asks a question or provides a statement to which the participants respond—and the *choices*—the possible responses to the stem.

BOX 2.7

Guidelines for Writing Statements
for Likert-Type Rating Scales

1. Write statements that contain one thought or concept.
   a. The career counselor helped me assess my career goals and make plans for implementing them.
   b. The career counselor helped me assess my career goals.
   c. The career counselor helped me make plans for implementing my career goals.

Statement a asks two things: about assessing goals and making plans to implement goals. Statements b and c are better: The respondent can rate, independently, how helpful the counselor was in assessing career goals and then in making plans to implement the goals.

2. Use familiar words and phrases.
   a. I advocate for persons who are unfairly chastised.
   b. I stand up for my friends.

Statement a contains words that are not frequently used and that are unnecessarily complex. Statement b is clear and to the point.

3. Write short, concise statements.
   a. I beseech of the teacher a succinct explication of the chronicle when parts of said narrative are incomprehensible to me and I require more comprehension.
   b. I ask the teacher to explain the story so that I can understand it better.

Statement a contains stilted and probably unfamiliar language—no matter what the target group! It's long, wordy, and confusing. Statement b uses familiar words and is much clearer.

4. Avoid proverbs and clichés.

    a. A stitch in time saves nine.

    b. Completing the Planning Phase of the survey project helped me create a better survey.

The proverb in Statement a is relatively well known . . . but will the respondent interpret the meaning as the survey author intended? Statement b is more to the point and is preferred.

5. Write unambiguous statements.

    a. Most politicians are a little bit corrupt.

    b. Taxpayers should not have to pay for the White House's Independent Counsel Investigations.

Statement a is ambiguous and confusing. Is it asking whether the respondent believes that most politicians are corrupt? Whether politicians in general are a little corrupt? And just what is "a little corrupt?" Statement b is not ambiguous and focuses on a related topic.

6. Avoid leading questions.

    a. Successful people agree that driving foreign-made cars is preferable. Do you?

    b. I prefer to drive a foreign-made car.

Statement b focuses on the respondent's preference for driving foreign-made cars. Statement a confounds the question about preference for driving a foreign car with its reference to successful people. Might respondents agree with the statement because they want to consider themselves successful?

(Continued)

BOX 2.7 Continued

7. Be inoffensive.

   a. Persons with physical disabilities think slowly.

   b. Persons with disabilities are very capable.

Both statements are offensive and suggest underlying stereotypes about persons with disabilities. The statements could be used in a measure of degree of stereotyped beliefs about persons with disabilities, but these kinds of surveys must be handled with great caution.

8. Communicate clearly to the target audience. (Survey about finances to welfare recipients)

   a. Aggressive growth mutual funds provide a better rate of return than CDs.

   b. It is important to me to pay all my bills each month.

Day-to-day financial survival is of concern to persons on welfare. They are likely to have little information about sophisticated investment vehicles; Statement a is inappropriate for this target group.

9. Ask for information or opinions that the respondents are likely to have. (Survey to students of a neighborhood school who walk to school)

   a. Long rides on the school bus each day make it difficult for me to stay awake in class.

   b. When I stay up late at night to watch TV, I have trouble staying awake in class the next day.

The survey author wanted to find out why students were sleepy and lethargic in class . . . but did not consider the type of school for the target population when she wrote Statement a. Statement b is appropriate for both neighborhood and commuting schools. Students at the neighborhood school don't ride school buses, so they do not have the experiences required to respond to Statement a.

10. Write statements at the appropriate reading and understanding level for the respondents. (A survey for third graders)
    a. I am dependable.
    b. My friends can count on me.

In Statement a, *the word* dependable *may be unfamiliar to some third graders. Statement* b *is preferred.*

11. Clearly address one of the objectives you've written for the survey.

    Objective: To determine the adolescent's attitudes toward the use of computers in composition writing.
    a. I look forward to time in the writing lab.
    b. I prefer to do my writing at the computer.
    c. I use the word processor for school-assigned writing only.
    d. Using the word processor makes it more difficult for me to revise my work.
    e. My work looks much neater when I use a word processor.

These five items all map to the objective and should provide you with a model for creating items that link to your objective.

12. Balance Agree-Disagree Items

    Balancing agree-disagree items helps ensure that respondents are reading the items and responding thoughtfully. In this way, respondents who tend to agree with all items must circle *disagree* for some items to consistently endorse a particular point of view.

(Continued)

BOX 2.7 Continued

The following items on opinions about various class activities provide an example. Read over the seven items carefully. Does this set of items have appropriate balance? (Note that respondents must *agree* with the positive items, but *disagree* with the negative to indicate satisfaction with the class activities.)

A = Strongly agree
B = Agree
C = No opinion
D = Disagree
E = Strongly disagree

1. I look forward to time in the computer lab.   A   B   C   D   E

2. I prefer to do my writing on the computer.   A   B   C   D   E

3. Group writing is a waste of time.   A   B   C   D   E

4. I look forward to small-group revision time.   A   B   C   D   E

5. I dread having my essays read by other students.   A   B   C   D   E

6. I think my writing skills have improved this year.   A   B   C   D   E

7. My peers usually give me good ideas about my writing.   A   B   C   D   E

Did you notice that this survey contained five positive items but only two negative ones? This is an example of what not to do! It appears the creator of the survey wants the respondent to think positively about the computer lab. You should have an equal number of positive and negative items in your survey; the negative and positive items should be placed randomly in the survey.

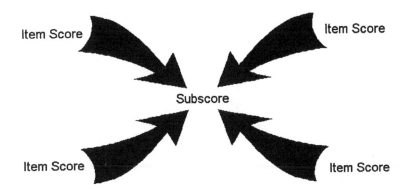

Figure 2.2. Combine individual item scores into a subscore.

Scoring Rating Scales

Scoring rating scales requires that you assign points to each of the anchors in a meaningful way. Here is an example of assigning points to anchors (SA = *strongly agree;* A = *agree;* U = *undecided;* D = *disagree;* SD = *strongly disagree*):

SA	A	U	D	SD
5	4	3	2	1

To obtain a "score" for one of your objectives, assign a point value to each choice the person has made, and sum the points. With the foregoing scale, a higher score indicates stronger agreement.

If you use a combination of negative and positive items, you'll need to flip or reverse the scoring for the negative items, as follows:

SA	A	U	D	SD
1	2	3	4	5

This scoring model is used with the negative items . . . where *agreement* means the person must *disagree* with the item.

You may want to compute subscores for each of your objectives, or you may want one total score. If you want subscores, sum the points for each of the items in that subscore. For a total score, sum the points for all the items.

Practice Activity 3:

Create a scoring system and score the following survey. Your scoring system should yield a higher score for agreement.

The Feelings Scale

Please read each of the statements carefully, then mark how you feel most of the time, by marking the letter that matches your choice. There are no right or wrong answers.
   Please use the following scale:

> A = Most of the time
> B = Some of the time
> C = Not very often

1. I am happy with myself.	[A]	B	C
2. Other children tease me.	A	[B]	C
3. I enjoy trying new things.	[A]	B	C
4. I get confused easily.	A	B	[C]
5. I can do anything when I try hard.	A	[B]	C
6. My schoolwork is too hard.	A	[B]	C
7. I don't like to raise my hand during discussions.	A	B	[C]
8. I feel important to my family.	[A]	B	C
9. Recess is fun.	A	[B]	C
10. I dislike school.	A	B	[C]

To have higher scores for agreement, use the following values for positive items (1, 3, 5, 8, and 9): A = 3, B = 2, and C = 1.

The following items will require "flipped" scoring: 2, 4, 6, 7, and 10, and the value for each of the anchors is as follows: A = 1, B = 2, and C = 3.

Did you compute 26 for the score?

Advantages of Rating Scales:

- They are familiar to most people
- The many variations of rating scales make them useful for many target audiences
- Scoring is relatively straightforward with a well-constructed survey

Limitations:

- Items must be carefully constructed to ensure you're getting the information you need
- High-quality items are time-consuming to construct

Semantic Differential Scale

The semantic differential scale is a combination of the adjective checklist and the rating scale. In this format, the single concept to be rated is written above the scale. Under the concept are a number of seven-point scales, with opposing adjectives or short phrases at each end, as shown in the following example.

How would you rate the use of a computer-based chat room to work on your survey project? Check the appropriate space on each scale.

Interesting	____:____:____:____:____:____:____	Uninteresting
Confusing	____:____:____:____:____:____:____	Clear
Useful	____:____:____:____:____:____:____	Useless
Efficient	____:____:____:____:____:____:____	Time-consuming
Boring	____:____:____:____:____:____:____	Fun
Worthwhile	____:____:____:____:____:____:____	Worthless
Inappropriate	____:____:____:____:____:____:____	Appropriate
Clear	____:____:____:____:____:____:____	Muddled

To construct a semantic differential scale, identify the concept about which you want opinions or feelings. Then, identify 8 to 16 adjectives that can describe the concept. Write the *opposite* of each of the adjectives.

BOX 2.8

Hint: Many word processors have a thesaurus tool that can help you here.

Randomly arrange the adjective pairs to help ensure that the respondent reads each pair carefully before responding.

Scoring

Scoring for the semantic differential and the Likert-type rating scales is very similar. Assign the values of 1 through 7 to the pairs of adjectives with the positive adjective on the right and the values of 7 through 1 to the pairs of adjectives with the negative adjective on the right. Sum the total number of points to obtain the score.

Advantages of the Semantic Differential Scale:

■ Provides an opportunity for the respondent to report feelings

■ Provides information about degrees of feeling

Limitation:

■ Measures feelings or opinions about only one concept

BOX 2.9

Guidelines for Writing a Semantic Differential Scale

1. Identify a concept that is related to one of your objectives.
2. Write 8 to 16 adjectives that can describe the concept.
3. Write the *opposite* of each of these adjectives (so you'll have 8 to 16 pairs).
4. Randomly order the pairs of adjectives, with half having the positive adjective on the right and half having the negative adjective on the right.
5. Separate each pair of adjectives with a seven-point scale.
6. Write the directions for the respondent.

The following table compares the advantages and limitations of the five response formats that have been discussed.

Review of Fixed-Response Formats

Format	Advantages	Limitations
Adjective Checklist	Easy to create	Cannot be scored to obtain numerical score other than number of adjectives selected
Behavior Checklist	Provides information about respondent's experiences	May be challenging to specify behaviors precisely
Ranking Format	Provides information about the relative standing of a set of items, activities, interests, and so on	Does not provide information about intensity
Likert-Type Rating Scale	Provides for a range of responses with a variety of anchors Provides a numerical score Can be used to obtain information on many topics	Scores in the middle range may be difficult to interpret
Semantic Differential Scale	Provides for a range of responses Can provide detailed information about a concept	Each set of scales is limited to one concept

Scoring Plans

You must have a scoring plan for your survey project, in which you provide instructions about how to assign points to each of your fixed-response items. We provided scoring information throughout the section on fixed-response formats, but we'll summarize it here.

Adjective Checklists

There are two ways to score adjective checklists, depending on the amount of detail you want. The first way is to count the total number of responses to positive adjectives and then count the number of responses to negative adjectives. The second way is to count the number of responses to *each* adjective. You can report results in a chart or table for either of these methods.

Behavior Checklists

Count the number of times each response (behavior) was chosen. You can report the results in a chart or table.

Ranking Format

Determine the average for each of the items on the list. The results are usually presented in a table that shows the items that were ranked, with the average ranking for each of the items.

Likert-Type Rating Scales

Review the discussion earlier in the text. When you created your rating scale, you decided on the number of anchor points. You must assign a numerical value to each of these anchor points. One example contains five anchor points; another has three anchor points. You may use three to seven anchor points for your rating scale. Generally, numerical values are assigned such that a high score indicates a higher level of agreement, endorsement, interest, and so forth. See Practice Activity 3 for details about assigning points to positively and negatively worded statements and obtaining a total score.

Semantic Differential Scales

Semantic differential scales are scored similarly to rating scales. Assign values of 1 through 7 to pairs of adjectives with the positive adjective on the right, and values of 7 through 1 to pairs of adjectives with the negative adjective on the right. In this way, a higher score will indicate a more positive endorsement.

Demographic Information

Do not assign point values to demographic items; these are not scored but rather are used to describe survey respondents and to form subgroups to help understand the data. (Details on demographic information are discussed in an upcoming section.)

BOX 2.10

For Your Survey Project . . .

Create specific scoring instructions for each question or statement in your survey.

Decide whether the survey items will be added together. For example, if items are measuring the same objective and have the same construction, they probably should be added together. Items measuring different objectives are *not* added together. Items that have different constructions (i.e., Adjective Checklist, Likert-Type Rating Scale) are *not* added together.

Describe what the scores mean. What does a high score mean? A low score? If you use subscores, tell what a high subscore means and what a low subscore means. (But do *not* try to interpret scores, such as 9 to 12 is high, 4 to 8 is medium, etc.)

Decide whether it makes sense to add all the subscores together to obtain a total score. What will a total score mean?

State the range of values for each subscore and for the total score (if you have one).

Collecting Demographic Information

What do you want to know about your respondents? Demographic information is collected for two purposes:

- To describe the characteristics of participants in the study

- To provide a way to form subgroups in order to make comparisons

What variables will help you understand the participants in the study? In the following list are some demographic variables that have been used in other survey research studies:

- Gender

- Age (in categories)

- Educational level

- Marital status of parents

- Birth order

- Grade point average (GPA)

- Environmental variables related to the research question

- Particular experiences related to the research question (e.g., attending summer school, participating in a leadership event, teaching in a year-round school, etc.)

Ask only for data that you will use! For example, you may want to investigate gender differences in your survey responses or differences based on certain experiences, such as participating in school clubs. In this case, you'll ask for gender and information about school clubs.

But you may also want to describe survey respondents with information about high school class (freshman, sophomore, junior, senior), GPA (by category), and the length of time the respondent has attended that high school. For this example, you'll have 5 demographic questions.

You must expect your target group to differ on your demographic questions. For example, do not ask for gender information if only women or girls are your target group. Or, if you administer a survey at the end of a workshop, you would not ask whether respondents have participated in the workshop!

To use the demographic information to look for differences, separate the completed surveys based on the demographic variable of interest, then summarize the information within these groups. You should have approximately even numbers of respondents in each of the categories of your demographic variables.

Demographic information is *not* scored but rather is used as descriptive information.

Writing Clear Directions

Clear directions:

- Let the respondents know exactly what you want them to do . . . check one response, check multiple responses, rank order several items, circle a response, write in a response, and so forth

- Are critical to making sure the respondents' answers to your survey are valid

Do not use the term "most appropriate" when you refer to a Likert-type response. This suggests to respondents that there are correct or preferred answers.

Place like types of items together, and provide directions for each set of items. For example, if your items use the Likert-type scale, with *agree-disagree* anchors, the directions might read as follows:

Read each statement and decide how much you agree or disagree with that statement. Circle the letter that corresponds to your answer, using the following key:

A = Agree strongly
B = Agree somewhat
C = Disagree somewhat
D = Disagree strongly

You may want to use a different set of anchors for a different set of statements, such as *frequency, satisfaction,* and so forth. *Each time you change anchors, you must provide a new set of directions.* Do not use two different sets of anchors on the same page of your survey.

Suppose the first five statements in your survey ask about the extent to which respondents agree with each statement, and the next five statements ask about the frequency of certain activities or feelings. Each of these sets of statements will require different anchors, so each will require a set of directions. Remember, each of these sets of questions (and anchors) will go on a separate page. In this example, the five questions with *agree-disagree* anchors go on one page. The next page will have the five items with frequency anchors.

Following is another example of directions for a frequency rating scale:

Read each statement and decide how often you feel that way. Circle the letter that corresponds to your answer using the following key:

A = Most of the time
B = About half of the time
C = Once in a while
D = Rarely

BOX 2.11

Important Reminder!

Put the anchors for the rating scale on the top of each page of your survey. Never assume that the respondents will remember your scale anchors or will know what you want them to do!

When in doubt about whether to include additional directions, err on the side of too much information. If your respondents don't understand what you want them to do, they may not provide valid information. And you won't know whether the respondents have become confused, because they are usually responding to your survey at their own locations, and all you see are their responses!

BOX 2.12

Important!

It is a good idea to include the following statement as part of the directions:

Completion of this survey is voluntary. By completing this survey, you are giving your consent to participate in this study. Completing this survey is completely voluntary and you may quit at any time.

Figure 2.3. Clear directions are a critical success factor!

Formatting the Survey Items

The format of your survey communicates important information to respondents. If the layout is pleasing, the directions clear, the typeface readable, and the items free of spelling and typographical errors, the message is, "I took time and thought to prepare this survey for you. Will you please thoughtfully fill it out for me?"

Layout

- Arrange the directions and items so the layout is pleasing, with sufficient white space so the items and response options are not crowded.

- Place rating anchors (if Likert-type scales are used) at the top of *each* page.

■ Provide separate directions each time you change item type. For example, if you have an adjective checklist, a semantic differential scale, and a series of items that use a Likert-type rating scale, *each* of these item types will require a separate set of directions.

■ Use double-spacing between items, but you may use single-spacing within the item.

■ Do not split an item over two pages.

■ If possible, use an ink-jet or laser computer printer with a scalable font. (A scalable font is one that allows you to change sizes and use bold or italics for emphasis.) Your presentation will look much more professional!

BOX 2.13

Be sure to include "Thank you for participating" at the end of the survey!

Skip Patterns

Skip patterns are used when some items will be answered by only a certain portion of the respondents. For example, you may want only respondents who have had certain experiences to respond to certain items. When this is the case, you'll format your survey so respondents without these experiences can skip these items. Be sure the directions are clear . . . so respondents will know exactly which items they are to answer. An example follows:

Skip Pattern Example

1. Do you have Internet access at home?

    (A) No (skip to Question 6)

    (B) Yes (please continue with Questions 2 through 5)

2. How often do you access the Internet for research purposes?

    _____ Once a week

    _____ Two or three times a week

    _____ Four or more times a week

3. How long is your average Internet session?

    _____ 60 minutes or less

    _____ 61 to 120 minutes

    _____ Over 2 hours

4. How often do you visit chat rooms?

    _____ Once a week or less

    _____ Two or three times a week

    _____ Four or more times a week

5. How likely would you be to access a chat room for help with your survey project if one were available?

    _____ Very likely

    _____ Somewhat likely

    _____ Not at all likely

6. Do you use the Internet from the library?

    (A) No

    (B) Yes

Reviewing and Revising the Survey

A peer review of your survey is in order at this point. If possible, two or more peers or colleagues should work with you to review your survey to help ensure its clarity and accuracy. Ideally, you have created a Survey Project Task Force during the Planning Phase of this project that can review the survey.

Step 1: Review the Questions for Clarity

Ask each peer reviewer to first complete the survey independently, as if he or she were one of the respondents, but do it using the following instructions:

1. Cover the choices and write out the answer.

2. Uncover the choices and see if your answer fits or matches one of the choices.

3. If your answer does not fit or match one of the choices, tell the author of the survey what your understanding of the item was.

4. If any of the items confuses you, tell the author of the survey what confused you.

5. If you have to make an assumption about what is being asked, tell the author of the survey what assumptions you made.

6. If you have any concerns about the survey, such as the way the items are asked, what experiences the respondent must have to provide valid responses, or the amount of reading or the reading level of the survey, discuss these concerns with the author of the survey.

Step 2: Review the Content of the Survey

Does your survey measure what is intended? Use the questions that follow to help you make sure your survey will gather the information you need.

Research Question and Objectives

1. What is the research question?

2. Do the objectives for the survey flow from the research question?

3. Is each objective stated in concrete terms?

4. Does each objective measure one idea or concept?

5. Is every item mapped to an objective?

6. Does every objective have a sufficient number of items to gather reliable information?

7. Does every item appear to measure the objective to which it is linked?

The Survey Items

1. Does the stem of each item contain only one idea?

2. Is the stem of each item clearly written?

3. Are there any grammatical clues in the stem or choices to suggest to the respondent a preferred or intended answer?

4. Do the choices provided represent all possible choices?

5. Do any of the choices overlap?

6. Do any of the choices lead the respondent to a particular answer?

7. Do any of the items appear to be biased in terms of race or ethnicity, age, handicapping condition, and so forth?

8. Does any item contain two negatives?

9. Is the order of the items balanced so the respondent is not always choosing the positive (or negative) choice to present a consistent position?

10. Are the demographic items appropriate to the target group?

11. Do the demographic items provide the information required to describe the survey respondents?

12. Do the demographic items provide the information required to form meaningful subgroups for summarizing the data?

The Target Group

1. Who are the members of the target group?

2. Are the items written so the members of the target group will have the ability to read, understand, and respond to each item?

3. Will members of the target group know enough about the topic to answer the items on the survey?

Step 3: Review the Overall Survey Format

Directions

1. Is there an overall set of directions for the survey?

2. Are all of the items using the same response format grouped together?

3. Are there separate and clear directions for each response format?

4. Is each set of directions clearly written?

5. Is there a set of anchors on each page that matches the items on that page?

Survey Format

1. Does the survey have a title?

2. Is the stem of each item longer than the responses to that item?

3. Are the item and its associated responses on one page and not split over two pages?

4. Are the choices in a logical order, such as alphabetical or degree of intensity?

5. Are there any typographical or spelling errors?

6. Are there any grammatical or punctuation errors?

7. Are the items numbered sequentially (and correctly)?

8. Is the overall layout pleasing, with sufficient white space and margins?

9. If skip patterns are required, are they correctly formatted?

10. If skip patterns are required, are the directions clear to the respondent?

11. Does the survey end with "Thank you for participating"?

12. Is there a planned use for all information being collected by the survey?

Step 4: Review the Scoring

Individually score the survey items you answered, using the scoring key provided by the author. Ask questions of the author if you don't understand what to do (and the author should take notes to clarify the directions for scoring).

1. How many points does each choice in each item get?

2. How many scores are calculated? (One total score or two or more subscores?)

3. Is each survey item included in one, and only one, subscore?

4. Does scoring information appear on the survey form the respondent will receive?

5. Has scoring been flipped (reversed) for items that were balanced?

6. What does a high score mean?

7. What does a low score mean?

8. Is there a subscore for each objective?

9. Overall, does the scoring make sense?

10. What is done with the demographic information?

Open-Response Items

An open-response item permits the respondent to provide a response rather than select one. Open-response items can be used to measure attitudes, interests, beliefs, opinions, preferences, experiences—in short, just about any topic about which you want to gather information.

Open-response items are used when:

- There may be a wide range of responses

- You would like to know the respondent's thinking about some topic, including reasons or details or both, that would be unavailable with a fixed-response item format

- You want more in-depth information than a Likert-type scale can provide

---

Sample Open-Response Items . . .

What fundraising activities should the PTA consider this year?
What facilities should the school district provide to support the use of computers?
In what ways can the workshop you just attended be improved?
What ways of structuring parent-teacher conferences do you find to be particularly effective?
What kinds of at-home instruction do parents of your students provide?

Open-response items are relatively easy to construct but require careful thought about the amount of time required of the respondent to provide a response. The items must be carefully worded to ensure they will provide the information you need.

Scoring

Scoring open-response items is a lot of work! Each response must first be read and then its key concepts identified. Similar concepts are then grouped into categories. In the fundraising example given in the sample questions, all activities should be listed, and when two or more respondents provide the same answer, tallies should be made of the duplicates.

In the example about structuring parent-teacher conferences, all the ways of structuring conferences should be listed. Sometimes, categorizing the responses requires judgment—are two respondents saying essentially the same thing but using somewhat different words?

Advantages of Open-Response Format items:

- Can be used to gather a wide range of information

- Permits respondents to express feelings, ideas, or reactions without being limited to preset categories

Limitations:

- Amount of time required to summarize the responses

- Amount of time that may be required for respondents to provide the information you need

- Requires that respondents be fairly verbal (so this format is not appropriate for young children)

Guidelines for Writing Open-Response Items

The guidelines for creating good open-response items are very similar to those for creating good statements for Likert-type rating scales. Comparative examples follow each point.

1. Do not ask leading questions.
    a. To what extent do you think involving parents in classroom planning activities creates too much extra work for the teacher?
    b. What role do parents have in planning activities in your classroom?

Question *a* suggests that having parents be a part of planning makes extra work for the teacher; Question *b* is more neutral. If parental involvement in planning does create extra work, respondents can so indicate, but they are not led to think in this direction.

2. Do not use loaded words or phrases that suggest approval or disapproval.
    a. Many teachers believe their workload is unfairly increased with the assignment of recess and lunchroom duty. What additional assignments have you been given this year?

      b. What responsibilities do you have in addition to teaching?

The word *unfairly* in Question *a* is loaded—it suggests that responsibilities beyond teaching are unfair. Question *b* is neutral and asks for information.

   3. Avoid social desirability in the questions.
      a. Successful teachers have found workshops such as the one we held today to be very useful. Did you like today's workshop?
      b. What was your reaction to today's workshop?

Question *a* suggests that because successful teachers liked the workshop, those teachers who consider themselves to be successful will also like the workshop. Question *b* is neutral.

   4. Avoid suggesting a response.
      a. How should teachers provide opportunities to students to make up tests they miss due to extended family vacations?
      b. What provisions, if any, do you make for students who miss tests due to extended family vacations?

Question *a* suggests that teachers should provide these opportunities—so a teacher may feel it necessary to create such provision. Question *b* allows for the possibility that teachers have chosen not to allow makeup tests.

   5. Encourage critiques by sharing a concern. An example follows:

      Some parents have suggested that their children have too much homework. How do you feel about the amount of time your child spends on homework each evening?

The question helps set the stage by indicating it's OK to have concerns.

    The following guidelines are very similar to those for rating items. Refer to that discussion for some examples.

   6. Ask for information the respondent is likely to have.

7. Write items at the appropriate reading and understanding level of the respondent.

8. Communicate clearly to the target audience.

9. Create clear and concise questions.

10. Clearly address one of the objectives you're created for the survey project.

Reviewing the Open-Response Items

Use the pilot testing and peer review procedures for these open-response items just as you did for the survey items. (We start with Step 5 here . . . you've already completed Steps 1 through 4 when you reviewed your fixed-response items.) If you're using only open-response items, start with these review questions.

Step 5: Review the Open-Response Items

1. What is the overall research question?

2. What are the objectives for the open-response items?

3. Are the questions neutral in form?

4. Do all questions meet the guidelines for good open-response items?

5. Do the open-response items appear on a separate page from the fixed response items in the survey?

6. Is there a plan for summarizing ("scoring") the responses?

Use Form 2.1, which follows, to make sure you're clear about the material covered by this chapter.

FORM 2.1

Phase 2 Checklist and Review

____ Were the appropriate types of items created to match the topic of the survey?

		Fixed-Response Formats			
Purpose of Survey Project	Adjective Checklist	Behavior Checklist	Likert-Type Rating Scale	Ranking Format	Semantic Differential Scale
A. Describe which extracurricular activities have the highest participation rates.					
B. Identify teachers' reactions to a proposed revision to planning periods.					
C. Describe the intensity of feelings about various plans for a post-prom party.					
D. Identify the most interesting stories to include in a literature unit.					
E. Describe the intensity of feelings about Internet access for classroom work.					

(See the next page for suggested answers.)

_____ Were the appropriate types of items selected for the target audience (considering age, reading level, knowledge base of target audience)?

_____ If you used a Likert-type rating scale, did you balance the agree-disagree items?

_____ Did you use skip patterns if certain respondents are to skip over some of the items?

_____ Does each objective have a sufficient number of items to provide reliable information?

_____ Did you identify appropriate demographic data elements to include in your study?

_____ Have you created a scoring plan?

_____ Is there a specific plan to use all the data you will collect?

_____ Are the directions clear and complete?

_____ If you are using open-response items, do they follow the guidelines for good items?

_____ Have you reviewed the survey items with peers or colleagues?

_____ Is the overall survey format pleasing?

Suggested mappings for fixed-response formats and purpose of survey project:

A. Behavior Checklist
B. Adjective Checklist
C. Likert-Type Rating Scale
D. Ranking Format
E. Semantic Differential Scale

Thomas, Susan J., Designing Surveys That Work! A Step-by-Step Guide. Copyright 1999, Corwin Press, Inc.

Figure 2.4. You've completed an important milestone for your Survey Project!

Phase 3

Obtaining Respondents

Phase 3 will help you pull together critical components of the survey project that will allow you access to your target group and to obtain informed consent from those who agree to participate.

In Phase 3, you will learn to create the following pieces of your Survey Project:

- Informed consent forms

- Letters to parents for consent (if required)

- Cover letters

- Gatekeeper letters (if required)

Informed Consent

Getting informed consent is just what it sounds like: providing information to potential respondents about the nature of the Survey Project and asking the person to agree to participate. The person must also know that once he or she has started completing the survey, he or she can stop at any time, without penalty. If you are working with minors, you must also receive the informed consent of a parent or guardian for the child to participate in the study. All of this is part of the *ethics of research.*

You must use an Informed Consent Form if

- Minors are being asked to participate in the study

- The topic is sensitive, such as drug or alcohol use or sexual or criminal behavior

- You have a power relationship over the respondents, such as your employees, your clients, or your students

You must have the signed Informed Consent Form *before* you give out the survey. If you require parent or guardian consent, you must have signed forms before your distribute the survey to the students.

If you are mailing the survey, include the statement about informed consent in the directions, as mentioned in Chapter 2. (*Completion of this survey is voluntary. By completing this survey, you are giving your consent to participate in this study. Completing this survey is completely voluntary and you may quit at any time.*)

Letters to Parents for Consent

A letter to parents is required if your target group consists of minors. The letter must contain the information in a cover letter (the description follows) as well as the information in the Informed Consent Form.

Parents need to know why their child is being asked to be in the study, what the study is about, when and where the child will fill out the survey, and who will have access to the information. Once this information is provided, there must be a space where the parents can sign, indicating that they give permission for their child to be invited to participate in the study. (The child can refuse to complete the survey even if the parent has provided informed consent.)

Cover Letters

A cover letter is written to motivate a respondent and is necessary for all surveys, whether they are sent through the mail or given to the person.

A cover letter tells

- Reasons why the person was chosen

- The purpose of the study

- Reasons the person should complete your survey (what's in it for her or him)

- Why the study is important

- About how long it will take to complete the survey

- When the survey should be returned (due date)

- How the respondents should return it (Prepaid envelope? Give to the teacher?)

- How the respondents can obtain a copy of the results (if you want to provide this option)

BOX 3.1

Motivating the recipient of the survey to answer your questions is a major challenge!

A good cover letter is

- Brief

- Informative

- Interesting

- Persuasive

- Motivating

- Personally signed by the researcher

The cover letter must sell the recipients on the importance of being part of your study. It must convince them of the importance of going from being *recipients* of your survey to becoming *respondents* to your survey!

- Never start a cover letter with "I"! Focus on the recipients of the letter and how they can benefit from participating in the study.

- Don't use words such as *hope* or *hopeful* . . . such as, "I hope that you will agree to participate." Use stronger words to encourage them to participate.

- Proofread the letter very carefully. Be sure there are no grammar, syntax, spelling, or typographical errors.

Some sample cover letters follow, with commentary to help improve them (and the response rate for the surveys!).

SAMPLE COVER LETTER 1

Dear Parents:

As a fellow parent of children in the Elmwood School District and as an individual concerned about the education of today's youth, I am requesting that you complete the enclosed questionnaire. The subject under review concerns reading instruction.

The questionnaire should require only a few minutes of your time to complete. The results of the data collected should provide valuable information concerning reading instruction. All of the families who participate in the survey will receive a summary of the results if they choose.

Your participation will help to satisfy requirements for a Master's Degree, which I am seeking from State University. Your cooperation is greatly appreciated.

Comments: In the first paragraph, the last sentence is stilted. Suggest combining with previous sentence: "... to complete the enclosed questionnaire about reading instruction."

What's going to be done with the information? What's in it for the person to complete and return the survey? Sounds like the only benefit is the student's course requirement being fulfilled. What does the respondent do with the survey when he or she completes it? When is it due back?

SAMPLE COVER LETTER 2

TO: All School and Rehabilitation Counselors

FROM: (student name)

I am a Special Education teacher with the XYZ Township School District and a graduate student at State University. My matriculation is in the field of counseling. I would like to specialize in and concentrate on counseling people with disabilities.

Comment: Sounds like the introduction of a letter of application for a job. The letter should focus on the respondent, not the researcher.

As a graduate student, I was asked to design a survey to collect data for one of my research courses. I have chosen the Metro County area of counselors for narrowing or isolating my data, focusing on Metro County alone; later, I would like to expand to other counties or states.

Comment: Communicates lack of interest in the survey; only reason for survey appears to be class assignment. Indicates Metro County has been chosen but no reason given. Expanding to other counties or states has little relevance to the respondent.

Your help in filling out this survey would be greatly appreciated and, in the long run, can help other counselors who are interested in helping those people with disabilities, as a lifelong career.

Comment: More on track but doesn't tell how these people will be helped.

This survey will take only a few minutes of your time to complete. A prepaid envelope is enclosed for the returned survey. If you have questions about the study, I will be happy to answer them. Thank you for your cooperation. Please return it as soon as possible or at your earliest convenience.

Comment: Need specific deadline. No phone number was included.

SAMPLE COVER LETTER 3

Dear Parents:

Enclosed is a survey that I am doing for a graduate class. The survey is on child care. It is an assessment of your attitudes toward child care and to find out if there is a need to start another child care program in your township. As many of you know, I have been coordinator of child care programs in your child's school for 2 years, in association with Good Charities. I chose the topic of child care for my research project because it is something that I really care about. I hope to incorporate the findings with my position at Good Charities to start a new after-school program in the winter. *All survey responses are confidential.*

> *Comment: First sentence communicates that the only reason for survey is a class assignment. More appropriate focus is on whether there is a need for another child care program. About choice of topic . . . one would assume that a research topic is something one cares about, and that fact should not be included in a cover letter. If the person's organization is for-profit, then there's a concern whether the information will be used to create a program for monetary rather than service reasons. Italics were in the original; there's no reason for italics to be used.*

A self-addressed stamped envelope is enclosed for your convenience. Please return on or before November 1. If you have questions or comments, you can contact me at my office between 9 a.m. and 6 p.m. at 777-7777, or use a separate piece of paper and include it with the survey. Thank you in advance.

Sincerely,

P.S. If you would like survey results, please request on bottom of survey, and I will mail them to you.

> *Comment: Good to give hours and phone number for questions. The postscript should be incorporated into the body of the letter. However, asking the respondent to put his or her name at the bottom of the survey breaks anonymity; there are other ways to accomplish this and still maintain anonymity of the responses.*

SAMPLE COVER LETTER 4:
AN EXAMPLE OF A MODEL COVER LETTER

Department of Teacher Education
State University
Statesville, New Jersey

October 1, 1999

Dr. Peter Germaine
Social Studies Department
Oceanside High School
South Beach, New Jersey 07191

Dear Dr. Germaine,

The Department of Teacher Education at State University pre-
pares over 100 student teachers every year to teach in the public
and private schools of New Jersey. It is our goal to help our gradu-
ates become as well prepared as possible to teach in today's
schools. The enclosed questionnaire is designed to obtain your
views on what we can do to improve the quality of our training
program. Your suggestions will be considered in planning for revisions to the program in the coming academic year. We will also
provide you with a copy of the results of our study.

We will greatly appreciate it if you will complete the questionnaire and return it in the enclosed, stamped, pre-addressed envelope
by October 15th. We realize your schedule is a busy one and that your
time is valuable, but we are sure that you want to improve the
quality of teacher training as much as we do. Your responses will
be kept completely confidential; we ask for no identifying information on the questionnaire form. The study has been approved by the
University's Research and Human Subjects Review Committee.

We thank you in advance for your cooperation.

Yours truly,

Dorothy C. Moore, PhD
Chair, Department of
Teacher Education

Obtaining Access to Your Target Group

Where is your target group? If your target group is high school students, you'll need permission of the school administration, the teachers involved, and perhaps the district's research unit. If your target group is clients at a counseling center, you'll need the support of the staff there to distribute and collect the surveys. In these situations (and many similar ones), you'll need a *gatekeeper letter* to request permission to obtain access to members of your target group.

There may be some survey projects for which you may not need special permission and a gatekeeper letter. These include using target groups where you can contact the participants directly, such as friends or members of a club to which you belong (you'll need to talk to club members but probably won't need a formal gatekeeper letter).

However, most of your survey projects will require gatekeeper letters. If you will need informed consent or permission from members of the target group, tell the gatekeeper how you will accomplish this. For example, if you want information from high school juniors about how they handle conflict in school, or their feelings about their families or things happening at school, you'll need informed consent from the parents or guardians before the students can be given a copy of the survey.

Results-Oriented Gatekeeper Letters

The gatekeeper may know you only through your letter and will judge you (and your project) accordingly. If your letter is sloppy, the gatekeeper may assume that the rest of your work will be sloppy also and will be unlikely to grant access to the target group.

- Use a business letter format
- Spell the person's name correctly
- Make sure there are no spelling, grammar, syntax, or typographical errors in the letter

A gatekeeper letter tells:

- Why it is important for the gatekeeper to agree to the study

- How much time will the survey take

- What the logistics are for doing the survey (Will their time and staff be required?)

- Why their organization was chosen

- What's in it for them

- What the purpose of the survey is

- What you plan to do with the results

- When you will contact them to answer any questions they may have about your project

There's no particular order for this information . . . just make sure the letter reads well and makes sense.

Include a copy of the survey with the gatekeeper letter so the person who can give you access to your target group will know exactly what you are asking members of the target group to do. (It's critical that the survey format be professional and free of errors!)

Following are parts of gatekeeper letters. Some have problems, whereas others have good points. The text of each letter is provided, then comments.

SAMPLE GATEKEEPER LETTER 1

Dear Guidance Personnel:

It has come to our attention that the individual counseling program currently in use in the district is not meeting the needs of our minority students. In order to develop a successful, multicultural group counseling program, we are asking that the students whose names appear on the attached list complete the enclosed questionnaire.

> *Comment: The survey author did not learn the name of the gatekeeper. The letter seems to be telling the guidance personnel they're not doing their job well, and there have been some complaints. (The names on the lists were those of students who had expressed an interest in multicultural counseling, per a note from the researcher, but there's nothing in the gatekeeper letter about why these students were chosen.)*

Please explain to the students involved that taking time and thought to respond to the questionnaire will help me in designing a group counseling program that will successfully address their unique needs.

> *Comment: Guidance staff have not been asked, and have not agreed, to help with the survey. It will be difficult for guidance staff to explain to students any details about the counseling program to be designed based on information in the letter. At this point, guidance staff do not know whether there is a need or interest in this type of counseling in their school.*

It is not necessary for students to identify themselves on the questionnaire. We do ask, however, that all questionnaires be completed in the company of a guidance counselor to ensure a high rate of return. Please return the completed questionnaires to the Board Office, c/o (name), by November 6.

Thank you in advance for your time and cooperation.

Comment: Guidance personnel are being asked to gather data for a study. What's in it for them? Will answers be valid if the student fills out the survey in the presence of a counselor? If students are told the questionnaire is anonymous, will they believe it? It seems threatening to return materials to the Board Office, especially with the entire burden of getting the student to cooperate being on the counselor. One can't assume they'll cooperate. We suggest that more details be provided about the study. The researcher should indicate he or she will call to answer questions and to discuss the school's participation.

SAMPLE GATEKEEPER LETTER 2

Dear Mr. X:

I am currently conducting research to examine the influence a teacher's clothing style can have on students' perceptions of teacher effectiveness. The study will take place in a junior-senior English class and would take two separate class periods followed by a student questionnaire. The 21-item questionnaire will ask for students' responses regarding their perceptions of teacher effectiveness. This information will be shared with all persons involved and can be used to plan more effective teaching strategies.

Comment: Good to indicate the purpose of the study, and how much class time it will take. A sample questionnaire should be attached to the letter. Because the study is about clothing styles and the researcher says the data will be used to plan more effective teaching strategies, does that mean a dress code might be implemented? Does sharing the results with all persons involved include the students?

SAMPLE GATEKEEPER LETTER 3

Dear Principal,

I am writing to request your cooperation and assistance in distributing the enclosed questionnaire throughout your school. As a master's degree candidate at State University, this will satisfy requirements for the course, "Introduction to Research."

Comments: Second sentence is not appropriate. Combine first sentence, rewritten so it doesn't start with "I," with the second paragraph.

The questionnaire is directed toward the parents of your students and concerns parental involvement with regard to developing prior knowledge and its relationship to the reading process. The questionnaire should require only a few minutes of the parents' time to complete. The data should provide valuable information concerning reading instruction. All families who participate in the survey, as well as yourself, will receive a summary of the results.

Comments: Provide more details on the anticipated benefits of the study. First sentence of paragraph is awkward and unclear, and should be rewritten.

I am hopeful that you will agree to participate in this survey and am looking forward to discussing its possibilities with you. I will contact you in the near future concerning the survey; however, should you need to contact me, please feel free to do so. I can be reached at 777-7777. Thank you for your cooperation.

Comments: Do not use "hopeful"! Suggest: I encourage you to participate in this survey . . . . Offer to call the principal in a week. Use the principal's name in salutation. How much time will the project take? Who distributes the survey? How is it returned? Who follows up? What direct benefit is there to the school?

Step Six: Reviewing the Ethics of the Survey Project and the Letters

Ethical considerations are an important element of a survey project. Work with your colleagues to be sure that you meet the research standards and ethical guidelines of your school district.

Ethics

1. Will the target group include minors? If so, is there a letter to the parent or guardian seeking permission for that child to take part in the study? Is there an informed consent form to be completed and given to the survey author that states the risks and gives permission for that child to participate in the study?

2. Is an informed consent form required? If so, is it included in the survey materials? Have the potential risks been identified?

3. Do the survey, gatekeeper letter, cover letter, and parent letter (if needed) make clear that participation is voluntary?

4. Is there a statement in the survey directions that completion of the survey gives consent to participate in the study?

5. What plans have been made to keep the survey data confidential?

6. Will surveys be returned anonymously?

7. Have survey participants been told that their responses will be anonymous or kept confidential?

Gatekeeper Letter

1. Does it use a business letter format?

2. Is it addressed to the head of the organization or institution, with the appropriate person named?

3. Does it ask permission to conduct the study on the premises of the organization (not assume it)?

4. Does it state the purpose of the study?

5. Does it indicate why the organization or institution was chosen for the study?

6. Does it indicate the benefits to the organization or institution for participating in the study?

7. Does it state reasons why it's important for the organization or institution to participate in this study?

8. Does it clearly indicate what the representatives of the organization or institution are to do? (Will they be required to set up rooms, have a janitor clean up after, use staff to administer the survey, etc.?)

9. Does it clearly state the amount of time the survey will take to administer?

10. Does it clearly state that participation of the respondents will be anonymous?

11. Does it indicate that participation of the respondents will be voluntary?

12. Does it indicate what the survey author will do with the results of the study?

13. Does it indicate when the survey author will contact the gatekeeper to answer any questions she or he may have about the project?

14. Is the letter free of grammatical, punctuation, spelling, and typing errors?

15. Does it indicate the survey author will contact parents for permission (if parental permission is required)?

Letter to Parent or Guardian (if necessary)

1. Does the letter explain the purpose of the study?

2. Does it ask for the permission of the parent or guardian for their child to participate in the study?

3. Does it tell how to return the informed consent forms?

4. Does it say what to do if there are questions?

Informed Consent Forms (if necessary)

1. Was the appropriate form from the school district used?

2. Are the known risks identified?

Cover Letter (to persons taking the survey)

1. Is the letter addressed to the recipient?

2. Is it written in language the recipient will understand?

3. Does it clearly state the purpose of the study?

4. Does it clearly state why the person was chosen to participate in the study?

5. Does it say why the recipient would want to complete the survey?

6. Does it say why the study is important?

7. Does it indicate how long it will take to complete the survey?

8. Does it clearly indicate *when* the completed survey must be returned?

9. Does it clearly indicate *how* the completed survey should be returned?

10. Does it indicate that participation in the study is voluntary?

11. Does it say that responses to the survey are anonymous?

12. Does it say how the respondent can learn the results of the study?

13. Will the survey author's method of collecting the names of people who want the results of the study destroy the anonymity of the survey?

14. What should the respondent do if he or she has questions?

15. Does the letter contain any grammatical, punctuation, spelling, or typing errors?

16. Has the author personally signed each letter?

FORM 3.1

Phase 3 Checklist

____ Have you identified a strategy to obtain Informed Consent forms from all participants?

____ Does your cover letter contain the important elements listed in the early pages of the chapter?

____ Will your cover letter motivate the survey recipient to become a respondent?

____ Do you need a gatekeeper letter? If so, does it contain all of the information listed in that section?

____ Have you attended to the ethical considerations of a Survey Project, including obtaining appropriate permissions?

____ What provisions have you made to ensure confidentiality of the survey responses?

Phase 4

Preparing for Data Collection

After many weeks of hard work, you are ready to put the finishing touches on your survey project. These include the following:

- Pilot testing

- Planning the data collection

- Producing the survey

Pilot Testing

Give your survey to two or three persons who represent the target group. These can be friends of yours or anyone who will help you out. Provide them the cover letter and the survey, as you would give it to members of the target group. Ask them to provide you with informed consent and then to complete the survey.

When they have finished responding, ask them to provide you with the following information:

- Were any items unclear? If so, which ones?

- Were the directions clear? Did you have any questions about what you were supposed to do?

- Was the cover letter interesting? Based on the information in the cover letter, would you be persuaded to respond to the survey?

- Is the format and layout pleasing?

- Do you have any suggestions for improving the survey or the cover letter?

The checklist to follow (Form 4.1) will help you keep track of the pieces of the Survey Project and will help ensure that you have all of the pieces before you begin data collection.

FORM 4.1

Survey Project Checklist

Materials that you will distribute to survey participants:

____ Gatekeeper letter (if used)

____ Permission letter to parents or guardians (if used)

____ Cover letter, on letterhead, as you will send it out to participants

____ Informed Consent form (if needed)

____ The survey

Title of the survey (descriptive but not biased)

Statement that participation is voluntary

Formatted as you'll send to participants

Materials that you will use for your final report:

____ Research question and objectives

Provide the research question that will guide your survey data collection.

List the specific objectives for the survey, with the question numbers for the survey listed next to each objective.

____ Scoring information: Include the details on how the survey will be scored

Planning the Data Collection

When you did the initial planning in Phase 1, you identified your target group: those persons who will respond to the survey and provide you with the data you need. You'll need to contact these people in order to gather your data.

- Provide detailed information about the people who will provide you the data.

    What are their characteristics? Are they members of some group, such as elementary school teachers in your district?

    Be specific in your description of the characteristics of the group, such as high school seniors at Wimberly School.

    How many people will you contact? What is your target response rate? (Remember that although you may send your survey to 100 people, not everyone will respond. If 30 persons return completed surveys, the response rate is 30%.) See Chapter 5 for more about response rates.

- Describe the process you will use to contact members of your target group.

    Do you have a list of names? What was the source of this list? Do you need permission to use the list? Is the list accurate?

    Do you have a contact person within the setting (such as school- or district-level personnel) that might be willing to distribute the survey for you (if this is appropriate)?

- Describe the process that you will use to distribute your survey.

    Will you use E-mail? A Web site? Face-to-face distribution at a meeting or workshop? U.S. mail? Campus mail?

    Do you have the appropriate permissions for the distribution method you'll use?

    If you're using an electronic distribution method (E-mail or Web site), do you have the appropriate permissions? Do you have the infrastructure in place to use this method?

Producing the Survey

After all the work you've put in so far, you're nearing the finish line! It's time to make copies of the survey (for mail or face-to-face distribution) or prepare the computer file for use on a Web site (for collecting the responses electronically). Making copies of your survey and cover letter and preparing the packages for distribution to potential survey respondents signals that you're ready for data collection!

Making Paper Copies

- Plan ahead so that when it is time to make copies, you're not lacking requisitions, purchase orders, or whatever you may need to get the copying done.

- If you're using a copy center, have you checked their requirements for turnaround time and the format they will need to make copies?

- Will you create individually addressed cover letters, perhaps with mail-merge software?

- Do you have the mailing list assembled? What plans do you have for addressing the envelopes or for preparing the return envelopes (if that's what you plan to use)?

- What plans have you made for stuffing the envelopes—putting the cover letter, survey, return envelope, and incentive (if used) into the envelopes?

Preparing for Electronic Distribution

- If you've decided to use an electronic distribution system, either E-mail or a Web-based mode, have you made arrangements for getting the survey into the appropriate format? Do you have the

E-mail addresses of the persons who are to receive the survey? If you are using a Web-based survey, how are you notifying potential respondents of the availability of the survey?

The checklist that follows (Form 4.2) can help you double-check the steps in Phase 4.

FORM 4.2

Phase 4 Checklist

_____ Did you conduct the pilot test and interview the participants to learn how you could make your survey even better?

_____ Do you have all the pieces of your survey project completed and ready to be produced?

_____ Do you have a list of persons who will receive your survey, either a mailing list or an E-mail list?

_____ If you're using E-mail or a Web-based delivery, do you have the infrastructure in place to make this happen?

_____ If you are using paper copies, have you have arrangements with a copy center?

Phase 5

Collecting the Survey Data

It's time to implement all of your planning and collect your data! You've created a survey to gather information for a specific purpose—whether for planning, making a decision, or understanding some aspect of human behavior. Every survey project has a deadline: the time when you need the data to do the planning or make the decision.

Figure 5.1. Time is of the essence!

Implementing the Data Collection Plan

In Phase 4, you created a process to distribute your surveys and the list of persons who will receive the survey. Now it's time to set that process in motion.

Your cover letter will include the following:

■ The due date for returning the survey

    All forms of survey distribution need this . . . including E-mail
    and Web-based surveys

■ Directions on how to return the survey

    Prepaid envelope? Return to a central location (such as at
    school)? E-mail address?

■ Any incentives you're providing to the respondents (such as a
  dollar bill in the initial mailing, something mailed to them on
  receipt of the survey responses, etc.)

■ The persuasive information described earlier that will convince
  participants to become respondents

Techniques for Increasing Your Response Rate

Despite all of your work in creating a high-quality survey, not everyone
who receives it will respond. Listed in the following table are some
techniques to increase your response rate.

Method	Optimal Conditions
Follow-up	More than one follow-up: Use telephone, additional survey (with an additional cover letter indicating this is the second contact), postcard reminder, E-mail note.
Inducement	Surveys containing monetary rewards often yield more responses—a dollar for a cup of coffee or a coupon for something. Sometimes, access to results or other professional material is also effective. E-mail or Web-based survey respondents may receive a reward on receipt of the completed survey.

Method	Optimal Conditions
Length of survey	Shorter surveys usually have better response rates. However, surveys over 10 pages also have good response rates with certain audiences.
Sponsorship	A cover letter inviting participation from a person the recipient knows produces good response rates. Institutional and professional organization affiliations also work well.
Cover letter	An altruistic appeal in the cover letter often produces good results.
Method of return	A stamped envelope usually works better than business reply mail. E-mail and Web-based surveys work best with some audiences.
Format	Aesthetically pleasing cover, interesting title, professional-looking layout, type that is easily readable, directions that are easy to follow, and skip patterns that work all contribute to higher response rates.

Following Up to Increase Your Response Rate

How many completed surveys are enough? The answer is—it depends! What is the size of the target audience? If it's fairly small, under 50, then you should try for the highest possible response rate. A 100% response rate is ideal, but try for at least 75%. You may require more than one follow-up reminder to attain this response rate.

With a larger target audience, representativeness is often more important that total response rate. If you are gathering demographic information to be able to summarize responses from different subgroups, you'll need to be sure you have enough respondents in these subgroups to have meaningful information. Many statistics books can provide you with formulas for computing the number of surveys to send out to obtain a good response rate—one that will provide enough information to support an informed decision.

sample of the organization. If you're planning advanced placement classes for high school seniors, gather enough information to make an informed decision.

Tracking the Survey Responses

You'll need some method of tracking the survey responses. If survey responses are anonymous, the only way to do follow-up is to send a reminder to all participants. It should both remind folks to complete and return the survey, if they've not already done so, and to thank those who have returned it.

As the surveys come in, start preparing the data for analysis and summary. You may choose to use a database for the survey responses by entering the data into a spreadsheet or creating tentative categories for the open-response items. In the next chapter, we show ways to create a data set in a spreadsheet.

Handling the Data: Confidentiality and Anonymity

As you gather information from your survey, it is critical that you respect the privacy of the individuals participating in your study. The two best actions to accomplish this are as follows:

1. Give the surveys anonymously. Instruct the respondents *not* to put their names on the survey. Provide this information in two places: in the cover letter and at the top of the survey (right under where you put the Informed Consent information). Do not write the person's name on the survey yourself.

2. Store the completed surveys in a locked and secure place. Only by breaking and entering should anyone be able to obtain these surveys.

Sharing the Results of Your Study

You may want to offer a copy of the results of the study to participants. Although it is not necessary to do so, it is a considerate offer to make. If you do make this offer, you must follow through!

- Obtain the names and addresses of those interested in receiving copies of the results. Keep this list in a separate location from the completed surveys.

- To maintain the anonymity of the surveys, ask those respondents who would like copies of the results to provide their names and addresses on a separate piece of paper. You can provide separate prepaid postcards for them to return to request a copy of the results or request forms that they can include with the completed survey.

Sharing With the Gatekeeper

You may decide *not* to offer respondents a copy of the results . . . and that's fine. But you must provide a copy of the results to the gatekeeper.

Here's another checklist (Form 5.1) to help you be sure you've completed the critical steps in Phase 5.

FORM 5.1

Phase 5 Checklist

____ What is the size of your target population? What proportion of respondents will you need for credible data?

____ Do you have a follow-up strategy to increase your response rate?

____ How will you protect the privacy of the respondents?

____ If you've offered to share the results of the study, how are you collecting the names and addresses of those respondents who want this information?

____ Have you made provisions to provide the results to the gate-keeper?

Phase 6

Summarizing the Survey Data

Phase 6 will guide you through the final steps of your survey project—summarizing the information you've gathered.

In Phase 6, you will learn to complete the following pieces of your survey project:

- Summarizing the survey results for the total group

- Summarizing the survey results for subgroups based on demographic data

- Describing the survey respondents

- Providing an answer to your research question

The suggestions presented here will focus on describing the information using percentages, averages, and charts and graphs. Some of you may wish to use more advanced statistical techniques to analyze your survey responses. No matter what techniques you use to summarize your data, two concepts are important: *variables* and *scales of measurement*. These are described in the following discussion.

Variables

A variable is something that can vary (have different values) along a dimension. A variable is anything that when measured, can produce two or more different scores. Examples of variables include age, gender, attitudes, how hard you work, the number of parents who participate in classroom activities, or the number of extracurricular activities available at the school.

Variables are measured with surveys. Results from a survey respondent (to a Likert-type scale) can be a value along a continuum, ranging from the lowest possible score to the highest possible score.

There are two important characteristics of variables:

- Continuous versus discrete

- Measurement scales

Continuous Versus Discrete Variables

A *continuous variable* is one that can take a variety of values, including decimals and fractions. Scores from Likert-type rating scales are an example of a continuous variable.

A *discrete variable* is one that is only whole numbers, numbers that may represent ranking or classification. Classification variables use numbers as labels, such as when we assign a number to a demographic characteristic.

Measurement Scales

Scores can be categorized in terms of the *scale of measurement*. Knowing the scale of measurement of your scores or data is important because it helps determine the appropriate statistical techniques to use. There are four scales of measurement:

■ Nominal—A classification. Numbers are used to identify groups with something in common. For example, flowers may be assigned numbers: roses = 1, daisies = 2, peonies = 3, pansies = 4, and so on. These numbers are simply labels and have no intrinsic meaning. For surveys, you may want to assign numbers to elements of your demographic data for ease in summarizing and reporting your results.

■ Ordinal—A rank order. Numbers are used to indicate relative standing. The ranking format described earlier provides rank order information about whatever items are ranked. In the example we provided earlier, participants were asked to rank the probability of success of various fundraising events for a PTA.

■ Interval—A measure of a specific amount, such as a test score. Data from Likert-type rating scales provide interval data.

■ Ratio—A measure of a specific amount, with an absolute zero. Physical measures are the best example of this scale of measurement, because zero is meaningful. Something can weigh nothing—and that's meaningful information.

Examples of Ways to Summarize Data From Surveys

To follow is an excerpt of a survey about reading strategies students may use as they read stories for pleasure. The survey was administered to a group of third-grade and fifth-grade students. A portion of the survey and a portion of the data are presented here for illustrative purposes.

Objective: To determine how strategic students are while they are reading.

A Likert-type rating scale was used, with frequency anchors as follows:

A = Most of the time
B = Sometimes
C = Rarely
D = Never

1. Before I begin reading a new book, I look at the pictures and title and try to guess what it is going to be about.

2. When I don't understand a part of the story, I just keep reading.

3. When I find a word in a story that I don't know, I read the sentences around it.

4. As I read, I can see pictures in my mind about what is happening in the story.

5. As I read a story, I ask myself questions about what will happen next.

6. I am confused by what I read.

7. When I get confused about a part of the story, I skip that part of the story.

8. I ask the teacher to tell me the words I don't know.

9. I think about what will happen next in the story.

10. I skip over words I do not know.

Scoring the Survey

Scoring: Items 1, 3, 4, 5, and 9 are good reading strategies; the anchors are assigned the following values:

A = Most of the time   4 points
B = Sometimes   3 points
C = Rarely   2 points
D = Never   1 point

Items 2, 6, 7, 8, and 10 are examples of poor reading strategies; the anchors are assigned the following values:

A = Most of the time   1 point
B = Sometimes   2 points
C = Rarely   3 points
D = Never   4 points

Coding Demographic Data

The following demographic data were collected:

Gender (girl or boy): We've coded girls "1" and boys "2". (These numbers are labels for categories to provide an example of nominal data.)

Grade level (third or fifth grade): We've coded third grade as "3" and fifth grade as "5." Again, these numbers are labels for the categories of grade level.

It's important to organize your data. You can use pencil and paper or a spreadsheet, such as Microsoft Excel or Lotus 1-2-3. This software will permit you to do simple calculations as well as create graphs and charts. We've used a spreadsheet to organize our sample data set, which follows. To recap, this is a partial data set from reading surveys that were completed by some third- and fifth-grade students.

A Sample Data Set

Respondent ID	Reading Score	Gender	Grade Level
01	18	2	3
02	22	1	3
03	25	1	3
04	33	1	3
05	21	2	3
06	18	2	3
07	17	2	3
08	16	2	3
09	24	1	3
10	26	1	3
11	19	2	3
12	14	2	3
13	26	1	3
14	28	1	3
15	26	1	3
16	25	1	3
17	27	1	3
18	24	1	3
19	21	1	3
20	31	1	5
21	29	2	5
22	32	2	5
23	34	2	5
24	36	2	5
25	36	1	5
26	28	1	5
27	27	1	5
28	31	1	5
29	25	2	5
30	22	2	5
31	28	2	5
32	26	1	5
33	31	2	5
34	35	2	5
35	36	1	5

Summarizing Survey Responses With Charts

Two examples follow, illustrating survey responses by using charts.

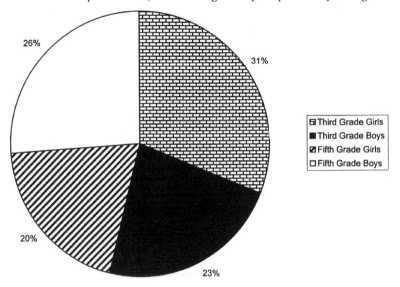

Figure 6.1. Demographic Data for Reading Survey

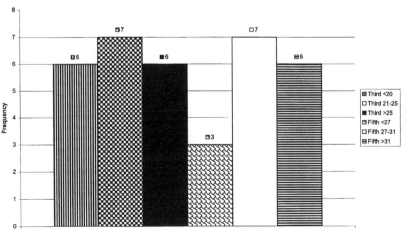

Figure 6.2. Reading Survey Scores by Grade Level

Summarizing Survey Responses With Statistics

The responses to the survey are examples of interval data, so they can be analyzed with a variety of statistical tests. In the following table, we've computed means by grade level and by gender within grade level.

Group	Third Grade		Fifth Grade	
	Number	Mean	Number	Mean
Girls	11	26.0	7	30.71
Boys	8	18.0	9	30.82
Total	19	22.63	16	30.44

Because the data presented here represent a part of the survey and a part of the sample, no conclusions are presented.

Summarizing Responses From a Survey That Used the Semantic Differential Format

Responses to a survey that used a semantic differential format are treated in the same way as those for the Likert-type rating scale described earlier. To follow is an example of a semantic differential item provided earlier. As with the reading survey example given, each survey respondent receives a score; data should be organized much as the example already provided. Because of its similarity in data analysis to the Likert-type rating scale, no data-based example will be provided here.

As a reminder, the following information was provided earlier about how to score responses from a semantic differential format:

Assign values of 1 through 7 to the pairs of adjectives with the positive adjective on the right and the values of 7 through 1 to the pairs of adjectives with the negative adjective on the right. Sum the total number of points to obtain an individual's score.

Demographic data are coded as in the previous examples.

In the example that follows, the person's response is marked with an "X." After the completed survey was received, the point value that maps to that response was added. Both pieces of information are provided in this example.

How would you rate the availability of a computer-based chat room to work on your survey project? *Check the appropriate space on each scale.*

Interesting	____:____:____:X(4):____:____:____	Uninteresting
Confusing	____:____:____:____:X(6):____	Clear
Useful	____:X(6):____:____:____:____	Useless
Efficient	____:____:____:____:X(2):____	Time-consuming
Boring	____:____:X(4):____:____	Fun
Worthwhile	____:X(6):____:____:____:____	Worthless
Inappropriate	____:____:____:____:____:X(7)	Appropriate
Clear	____:X(6):____:____:____:____	Muddled

Summarizing Responses From a Survey That Used a Ranking Format

The following table is the example ranking scale provided earlier, with responses from one of the respondents.

Please rank the following PTA fundraising activities in terms of their potential for success in our community. Assign "1" to the activity you believe will be the most successful, "2" to the activity you believe will be second most successful, and so on.

Activity	Ranking
Car wash	2
Bake sale	5
Silent auction	1
Concert	3
Dinner dance	4

Unlike the process used to summarize responses from Likert-type rating scales and the semantic differential format in which scores for each respondent are computed, responses to the ranking format are summarized by group. If you use subgroups based on demographic information, average rankings are reported for each of the subgroups, as well as the total group. As a reminder, here is a portion of a ranking-format survey.

The following format is useful for organizing the responses and includes data from the preceding example:

ID	Item 1	Item 2	Item 3	Item 4	Item 5	Demo-graphic 1	Demo-graphic 2
01	2	5	1	3	4		
02							
03							
04							

Data in the cells are the rankings provided by each of the respondents. Average rankings are computed for each item, either for the total group or for subgroups based on the demographic data.

Communicating the Results of Your Survey

You've successfully completed your survey project! You now have information that you can use to plan, make decisions, identify needs, or describe behavior or attitudes.

Think about how to present your findings. Consider the audience that will be receiving the information. Identify your key findings. Often, charts and graphs communicate best. Some people are put off by lists of numbers and lots of reading. A high level overview with details available for those interested is usually the best approach. When you present your findings, you should have available the complete survey package (survey, cover letter) to show interested audience members.

**CORWIN
PRESS**

The Corwin Press logo—a raven striding across an open book—represents the happy union of courage and learning. We are a professional-level publisher of books and journals for K–12 educators, and we are committed to creating and providing resources that embody these qualities. Corwin's motto is "Success for All Learners."